FEB   2019

French COUNTRY

WITH CHARMING, TIMELESS INTERIORS

French COUNTRY

WITH CHARMING, TIMELESS INTERIORS

CINDY SMITH COOPER

83
PRESS

Hoffman Media
1900 International Park Drive, Suite 50
Birmingham, Alabama 35243
hoffmanmedia.com

ISBN # 978-1-940772-54-7
Printed in China

83
PRESS

Contents

INTRODUCTION

Anyone who has traveled the French countryside has undoubtedly been struck by its profound beauty. Those of us who picture it only in our dreams can almost as easily envision the exquisite brilliance of the gently rolling landscape and the lovely French farm-style homes filled with timeless charm and the warmth of tradition and family memories. For decades, homeowners across America have aspired to capture the allure of French country style. For whatever reason, this captivating aesthetic speaks to us deeply as a heartfelt expression of hearth and home. To many of us, the style offers a haven of serenity, where life is blissfully comfortable, pared down, and unpretentious.

The picture of understated elegance and impeccable charm, French country style is a look and a lifestyle originally inspired by the modest stone farmhouses of southern France. Celebrating the vibrant and beautifully sun-drenched colors of Provence, this abundantly inviting style exudes a kind of relaxed elegance and effortless ease that epitomizes the spirit of the French interior. Today, it is as prevalent in the city as it is in the most remote rural areas, and Americans especially have taken to it with exuberant joie de vivre.

French country charm can certainly mean many things to many people. At its best, it is a visually balanced and artful layering of generously proportioned furniture, sumptuous fabrics, delightful textures, and eye-catching patterns that, when combined together, create a calming sense of comfort.

Modest or majestic, the architectural style and embellishments of a house can vary from region to region, but for the purist, distinctive features, including cobbled courtyards, rough-sawn wooden posts and lintels, quoins, stone window sills, magnificent stone fireplaces, rustic ceiling beams, and rounded wall corners are sure to lend authenticity and a rural vernacular to any dwelling, no matter the setting.

Welcoming and livable spaces are sprinkled with individuality—the pieces themselves often characterizing the personalities of the homeowners. Rooms come alive with walls that are simply papered, handsomely upholstered, or cleverly painted with trompe l'oeil techniques and decorative finishes that create a sense of age and well-worn patina. Family photographs and treasured heirlooms passed down for generations mix graciously alongside quirky flea market finds and cherished collectibles. An abundance of fabric spills forth everywhere, softening rough edges and bringing inviting comfort to every space. Luxurious draperies bearing dressmaker trims such as piping, fringes, tiebacks, and tassels cascade from windows large and small, bringing Old-World elegance to even modestly scaled rooms. Delightfully simple and sheer, or exquisitely tailored and grand, fabric embellishments are applied with artistic aplomb—draping across tables, upholstering bedroom and powder room walls, adorning lampshades, billowing from canopy beds, or adorning tiny cottage windows with just a thin veil of lace. Rustic floors—lustrous hardwood, glossy tile, and ancient stone—are covered in delightfully textured rugs made of elegant seagrass or chunky sisal, and stunning antique wovens—Aubussons, Savonneries—look as though they may have been plucked from a stately French château or a humble farmhouse, or *bastide*.

But how exactly do we combine all these elements with the same effortless style and graceful panache as the French? Certainly, from a decorator's standpoint, we can adhere to some of the key fundamentals of design, such as scale, proportion, texture, and color, to properly emulate French country style. But perhaps the real beauty stems from a lack of rules and a personal freedom of expression that ensures personable charm, a uniqueness of lifestyle, and a sense of individuality in the inhabitants and their collectibles. By applying just a few surefire techniques—a joyful mix of color and pattern, elegant rustic finishes, a pleasing blend of classic and contemporary, and a whimsical layering of refined objects and eclectic curiosities—any room can evolve quite naturally into a blissful, French-inspired tableau of meaningful finds that reflects your truest expression of hearth and home.

Keeping CHARACTER

Gloria and Eric Stewart have restored a number of houses since they moved to southwest France nearly 30 years ago. Their restorations are always a magical blend of flair and sensitivity. When they decided to move in 2009, it was to trade a large house for somewhere smaller. This 18th-century farmhouse, high above a valley in Périgord, offered a majestic view, but behind its stone walls was an empty shell. Until the Stewarts acquired it, the house had not been occupied for more than 35 years, and before that, only in two ground floor rooms, as there was no upper floor. The rest of the long building consisted of two barns, one a tobacco drying chamber, and both with earth floors. The roof had been maintained, but there was no sanitation.

To turn this blank canvas into an authentic 18th-century interior, the Stewarts approached it in their usual way, as Gloria explains. "We always decide on the criteria that will suit how we will live in a house. Here, we wanted a large kitchen with a fireplace, a dining room, and a large living room. Upstairs, we needed three bedrooms, one en suite, and an additional bathroom. This part was tricky because we were building into the roof space. On the other hand, the house and barns are in a straight line—there's nothing higgledy-piggledy—so running electrics and plumbing wasn't complicated.

A terrace was added to the side of
the house, looking along the valley.
"We love to eat out here in summer
and watch the sunset," says Gloria.

We worked with French builders who were sympathetic with what we were doing, but it was 18 months before we could move in."

The plans Eric drew up gave them a good-size kitchen by knocking down the wall between the two once-occupied rooms. Some of the space released became a laundry room and a small corridor into the first barn. This barn was divided into an entrance hall with a staircase to the new first floor and a dining room. Introducing a large window and a little balcony in the dining room not only offers up a fine view across the valley but introduces natural light that spills over into the rooms on either side. The second barn, the one used for tobacco drying, became their large living room, and Gloria and Eric sourced 18th-century glazed double doors to fit between the two rooms. A feature of Eric's plan is the enfilade. This tradition in French architecture aligns rooms and doorways, giving a long perspective—in this case, from the living room right through to the kitchen.

The space for rooms in the roof was more limited, as the second barn was only one story high. "Ceiling height was a problem in the roof," Gloria agrees, "and we had to chop out some of the timbers so that we don't bump our heads when getting into bed."

In describing their approach to the restoration, Gloria credits Eric as being skilled in seeing the optimum way to reorder space. "What's important to both of us," she says, "is keeping a sense of what the building was and not trying to make it into something it is not. There was nothing architecturally interesting about this building beyond the character of the shell. I always kept in mind that this is a farmhouse, and though it dates from the 18th century, which is my favorite period, we've tried to temper any tendency to grandeur—for instance, by putting wood cladding on some of the ceilings and the living room walls, a feature we have seen in modest buildings in this area. Whenever there has been an opportunity to install reclaimed materials, including doors, fireplaces, and floor tiles that match the period of the house, we have sourced them from reclamation yards. Things like this are not difficult to find here if you know where to look, but each year, they become less affordable."

The decorative finishes Gloria has chosen are simple, even rustic, though the furniture, pictures, and textiles she has collected during the time they have lived in France add distinction to every room. In each house they have restored, Gloria always has a fireplace installed in the kitchen if there is not one there already, and Eric tracked down the one for this kitchen in a reclamation yard near Paris. It dates from around 1800 and, by coincidence, is carved with the same sunflower motif that is a feature of the marriage cabinet from Normandy that stands next to it. "To keep control of our budget," Gloria says, "we bought kitchen cabinets from Ikea but modified them to suit the room by distressing the fronts with paint, adding old handles, and fitting an oak work top."

The furniture, textiles, and muted colors that run throughout the house reflect Gloria's love of 18th-century decoration. She purchases her sofas and and some of the chairs in England, preferring the custom of sinking into large, roomy sofas rather than sitting upright in more traditional, formal seating. Of course, it is not just comfy sofas that sum up the charm of this restored farmhouse. As Gloria explains, "With its interconnected rooms, this is a house for easy living, and that was always our plan."

Gloria found the side table in one of the barns, and its soft gray patina blends with the colors in the room. The pictures on the boarded wall are 18th-century chinoiserie, and the painted box is a Swedish antique. French doors to the garden have replaced the original barn doors, which have been reused as the entrance gate. Curtains with an embroidered sprig motif are by Chelsea Textiles, and the chair is covered in a 19th-century print.

The lower walls in the living room are clad with pine planks color-washed in "French Gray" with vertical planks on the upper walls in "Clunch," both by Farrow & Ball. They first established symmetry in the living room by arranging a pair of doors found at a reclamation yard. Fitted over front alcoves, the doors cleverly conceal household linens on one side and a television on the other.

ABOVE: The 18th-century Swedish desk in the corner of the living room is unusual in incorporating a clock and a secret drawer. It has retained its original paint.

OPPOSITE: Eric sourced the 18th-century half-glazed doors between the living and dining rooms. Cushions on the sofa are covered in a mix of 18th- and 19th-century printed cottons and embroidered linens from Chelsea Textiles. An early Indian shawl covers the chair seat.

The dining room doubles as a library. It is furnished with woven chestnut chairs, which are still made in the Périgord region. The 18th-century wall sconces were found at antiques fairs. The dinner plates are 19th century, and the antique monogrammed napkins were dyed to a soft gray by Polly Lyster.

OPPOSITE: The kitchen ceiling is boarded with rustic planks to contain the height, a theme running through several rooms. Walls are painted in "String" by Farrow & Ball.

BELOW: Gloria displays ceramic treasures in an antique marriage cabinet. The chair is upholstered in a 19th-century blue-and-white check. The 18th-century figure holding a bowl for salt is one of Gloria's favorite pieces. She found the decorative paper shelf edging at a *brocante*, or flea market. The reclaimed fireplace has the same carved sunflower motif as the marriage cabinet, suggesting that both came from the Normandy area.

OPPOSITE: All the bedrooms are tucked into the roof space. A little French quilt is thrown over a white figured coverlet from Cologne & Cotton.

RIGHT: The boarded floor in the guest bathroom was color-washed and sealed. The blind is made up in a typical 19th-century bird print. The caned chair is also 19th century.

OPPOSITE: Walls in this guest bedroom are papered with some rolls of 19th-century American hand-blocked wallpaper that Gloria bought at an antiques fair. A sheet dyed by Polly Lyster has been converted into a valance, and the 19th-century crocheted bedcover is from the Provence region.

French FLAVOR

Both visual artists at heart with a zest for living the good life, Patrizia Maffeo and her husband, Dario Polenghi, eagerly uprooted their lives in Italy to embark on a historic journey in the South of France. Proprietors of an antiques atelier and interior design business in Milan for many years, the adventurous couple just couldn't resist the challenge of restoring an ancient farmhouse when the opportunity presented itself. Set amid the countryside of the Petite Camargue, a region of southern France between the Mediterranean Sea and the two arms of the Rhône delta, the old farm, or *Mas de Bony*, as it was named, dates back to the mid-17th century. At the time of its construction, it represented an important communication route linked to the trade of the precious salt that came from the nearby salt marshes located on the coast of the Mediterranean Sea.

"The guiding thread of our dècor for the Mas de Bony was closely linked to the origins of the original construction," says Dario. "Our interpretation of the restoration needed to honor the nature and origins of this place but also address the needs of a more modern lifestyle. Our choice of colors and materials were performed in compliance with these parameters but were also infused with personal taste, the need for updated comforts, and a certain aesthetic aimed at the French country spirit," he notes.

Assisted by Dario, Patrizia took the lead as the interior designer for this endeavor. She first selected the decidedly varied yet balanced color palette that ranges from pink-periwinkle to ice green tinged with hints of gray and light yellow. The subdued color of the walls was achieved with a lime wash, a technique that creates a soft patina with natural color variations. The structural restorations were all done with stones and woods of the region, and fabrics were chosen to blend with and balance the color palette.

"We also emphasized the context in which these choices were made," says Dario. "We considered long and sunny summers, short and mild winters, ordinary people and cheerful friends, great relationship life, lunches and dinners in joy, a company of friends always willing to organize parties with music, dances, simple food but great quality, and above all, many reflections and positive thoughts," he adds.

Now enjoyed as the couple's holiday home, the Mas de Bony exudes the kind of rustic elegance that epitomizes the southern French lifestyle. The interiors are a work of harmony—the colors, fabrics, and furnishings mix seamlessly without jarring contrast. Special pieces nod to the storied history of the farmhouse, including the sacristy that is lacquered and painted with religious figures, and a wooden bathtub created from a wine barrel that commemorates the cultivation of the vine and the production of wine that was once the main activity on this property. Other original furnishings include tools necessary for the work of the farm—an ancient zinc bath for washing, an implement for raking the ground, and a rotating wooden bucket that was used for the production of butter immediately after milking the cows. Exquisite original pieces, such as a long sofa once used for afternoon siestas and a large series of Gien and Sarreguemines dishes that hang on the walls, embody the very essence of the Provençal spirit. On the back of the building, there is a fenced garden where five towering sycamore trees sway in the breeze. On warm summer days, they offer cool shade and the sweet song of cicadas.

"This is absolutely our favorite place—where we and our guests love to relax and take advantage of the idyllic atmosphere," says Dario. "This is perfectly southern French country."

PREVIOUS PAGES: The dining room wall, covered entirely with an exquisite service of creamware dishes, makes a compelling display. A French country lacquered bench creates an eye-catching contrast against the striking green wall. In the dining room, a 19th-century lacquered wooden sacristy from the South of France honors the storied history of Mas de Bony, an ancient 17th-century farmhouse that was recently restored by Dario Polenghi and his wife, Patrizia Maffeo. Ceramic and porcelain pieces of various origins compose a captivating wall vignette that complements the rustic yet elegant interior.

ABOVE AND RIGHT: The walls of the dining room are painted with a lime wash, which generates a patina that softens and stirs with subtle movements and natural color variations. A collection of chinoiserie ceramics artfully arranged on the wall creates a captivating focal point.

LEFT: A grand stone staircase leads to the upper rooms and library, as well as a lower interior courtyard. The walls are gracefully embellished with white relief pieces and images of shooting stars, artwork that was rendered by homeowner Dario Polenghi.

OPPOSITE: An antique settee complements the stone walls and rustic wooden ceiling beams of this apartment annex at Mas de Bony that overlooks the country fields.

BELOW, LEFT: Ancient tiles and a quirky painting of two herring are just a few of the whimsical accents that bring charming personality to Mas de Bony's kitchen.

OPPOSITE AND THIS PAGE:
Filled with natural light, a serene room between the kitchen and the dining room holds antique storage pieces, including a wardrobe with its original Louis XIV lacquered doors that is used to house serving pieces and other tableware embellishments. An ancient terra-cotta olive oil jar, a 19th-century iron table, and a French country armchair add to the room's Old-World charm, as do the creamware dishes and three delicate paintings that adorn the walls.

OPPOSITE: A country-style shower in the large guest room is composed of an antique tap and a tub crafted from an old wine barrel.

LEFT: A collection of antiques recalling the history of the farmhouse, including tools once used for working in the fields and an old butter churn, compose an alluring vignette against the stone walls of the upper patio.

Old Farm, NEW LIFE

American/Dutch couple Jitske and Matthew Poventud arrived in France with their three young children and a dream. "We were always busy, but in our hearts, we longed for another kind of life. We wanted to spend more time with our kids and with each other," Jitske says. They decided to follow their heart and began searching for a place to live their dream—a place where they could live and work at the same time. On top of their wish list: a place of silence, quiet and unspoiled.

After nine months of viewing houses in the Netherlands, Belgium, and northern France, Jitske discovered aerial photos of Château de Digoine, a magnificent medieval estate in the Burgundy region that had been neglected since World War II. The couple soon found themselves standing at the centuries-old gate that marks the entrance. Jitske and Matthew describe a rainy introductory tour of the grounds, during which they used flashlights, as all of the shutters were closed. The last owner left the estate just before World War II, and during the war, monks lived inside. After the war, it remained uninhabited. There were thousands of antique pieces in it, ranging from tables, chairs, and cabinets to cutlery, books, glassware, and clothes. Despite the less-than-ideal conditions, the Poventuds could see something grand. "It was such a beautiful, noble building," Matthew says.

OPPOSITE: Dinner is served in the private living room in the main house. The fireplace and mantel are original to the house, and the antique wine bottles were discovered in the castle's cellars.

ABOVE: Jitske always takes great care in setting the table, using her collection of Sarreguemines *Royat* tableware, which she combines with colorful glassware and contemporary ceramics from local artisan Ine Schoots. The sandstone arch in the kitchen was discovered during the renovation of the house.

That afternoon, the couple became the owners of a castle, two houses, a 19th-century chapel, several barns and stables, a hunting lodge, an orangery, a watermill, a lake, and a forest.

"We started this adventure with the idea of finding a home first, and after that, deciding how to earn our living," says Jitske. "This could have been anything, as long as we could work at home and be with each other as a family as much as possible. Soon after purchasing the estate, we got the idea of starting a guesthouse. We could live in the main house ourselves and create guest rooms in the other house across the courtyard." Both houses were built between 1810 and 1820. They had been uninhabited for many years and were in need of serious renovation. Many windows were gone, and the buildings were overgrown. The roofs were in good shape, and there were many authentic elements left, such as the old *tomettes* (traditional floor tiles), a huge sandstone fireplace with a bread oven, a marble mantelpiece, a sandstone winding staircase, and a wooden roofed staircase outside.

"Because the houses were built in function of the castle, only the best building materials were used," says Matthew. "While renovating, we even discovered that there were only square angles, which is unique." Also unique are the huge window openings in every room, framed with sturdy sandstone blocks. "Normally, in old French houses, you'll find one or more windowless walls, at least on the northern side," says Jitske. "There's so much light coming in, and there are superb views from every room: the kitchen garden, the castle, the courtyard…it feels like being outside, even when you're inside."

Although the Poventuds had three small children and a lot of animals to take care of, Matthew and Jitske renovated everything themselves, now and then assisted by family and friends. Their priority: having the guest rooms built in the *Maison de Gardien*, once the caretaker's house. The *gardien*—who also was responsible for the horses—lived on the first floor. The ground floor originally housed horse carriages. Upstairs were five small rooms, a bathroom, and a kitchen. The Poventuds transformed the ground floor into a light-filled, shared living room and breakfast area. They reconfigured the upstairs into four comfortable bedrooms (named after previous owners of the estate: Humbert de Musy, Guillaume de Damas, Charles de Prunelé, and Henriette de Faletan) with adjoining luxury bathrooms.

Later, Matthew and Jitske recast the circa 1810 hunting lodge, once home to the gamekeeper, as a *gîte*, or guest cottage, and completed all restoration using building materials original to the estate. They added a two-floor extension covered with cedarwood. It houses a spacious kitchen and a superb bathroom, both with large windows and glass doors opening to the abundant nature outside. There is also a magnificent mantelpiece with an interesting backstory. "One day we found a beautiful carved stone in the vegetable garden," Jitske recalls. 'When digging further, we found many more. They appeared to be part of a 14th-century mantelpiece! Only the cornerstones were missing, so we made those ourselves."

Whenever the couple needed building materials, they looked outside and in the barns. They reused old doors, handles, and wood. They built the outside stairs of the hunting lodge using stones from a ruined building, and the wooden flooring in the guest rooms was made from eleven Douglas firs harvested on the property. They had the trees sawn at the local wood mill, but they made the planks themselves.

Like the grounds and barns, the castle also became a treasure trove for finding all the decorations needed in the guesthouses. Being faithful to the robust base of the buildings, they used strong materials such as old wood, massive oak, and rough stucco. They added warmth and elegance with antiques from the castle and *depot ventes* (sales depots), and with high-quality patterned textiles and curtains. Sometimes they added a modern counterweight through contemporary pieces of furniture and bright colors, like the bright blue painted on some walls. "It's often the wall behind the bed that is painted," says Jitske. "In this way, a color never comes at you." Great care is taken that rooms never get over-decorated. "The focus should be on all the beauty outside," she says.

When they're not busy being great hosts for their guests, Jitske and Matthew take care of their children, their animals, their garden, and their forest. They maintain the castle to save it from total collapse, and they just finished transforming the orangery into a new guesthouse. There's never a dull moment, and they love it. "We want our guests to experience life on this estate, the nature, and the tranquility," says Jitske. "Many people tell us coming here feels like coming home—and that's a wonderful compliment."

LEFT: Unstained oak, bright blue walls, and classic Thonet chairs bring a contemporary touch to the rustic bones of the shared living and breakfast room. The homeowners crafted the wainscoting, using oak from their own forest. The stone floor was already there, as were the beautiful old doors, once leading to the tack room—now a shared pantry.

BELOW: Ceramics made by Ine Schoots, a Dutch artist living near Château de Digoine.

OPPOSITE: A close relative of the former owner of the castle donated old cadastral maps, depicting the estate property in 1898.

LEFT: Glass doors in the combined breakfast/living room open onto the lovely natural scenery surrounding the courtyard, where diners can linger with a glass of wine.

The former hunting lodge was once home to the estate's gamekeeper and his dogs. Now guests can relax in this comfortable living room with its authentic vaulted ceiling and robust fireplace. The stones around the fireplace originate from the castle. The modern kitchen seen at the right was built into the new extension.

LEFT: Guest room Chambre de Faletan is located on the ground floor. The floor planks were made from cedar trees harvested on-site.

OPPOSITE, LEFT: Beautiful glassware found in the castle adds a subtle accent of color and charm to the room.

French
LOVE AFFAIR

Wind your way up a steep cobbled street, dappled with Mediterranean light and hedged in by tall, sun-bleached stone houses with geraniums cascading over window boxes, and you come to a creamy yellow façade adorned with grey-green shutters. The house, which Jean and Doug Hill bought, is part of the terrace built into the old 12th-century village rampàrts and famously used as a lookout post by the Germans in the Second World War.

"You can see why they wanted it," Doug says as he observes the breathtaking view from the roof terrace. "On a clear day, you can see from the Côte d'Azur to the Italian border." The fact that the house was used as a lookout post proved a major problem. The weight of the fortifications had pushed the façade outward, and below it, the house was slowly collapsing, although previous owners had lived there for many years, oblivious of the dangers.

Despite these structural problems, the Hills took the plunge. "We just fell in love with the village and the position of the house. It was the third-highest in Mougins, with a rooftop terrace, high ceilings, and good room sizes. The potential was huge, and the timing was right. Our two girls Betty and Daisy had finished their English education, so we were free to fly."

PREVIOUS PAGES: Sofas are grouped around the coffee table, adapted from a 19th-century Indian bed in the sitting room on the raised ground floor.

RIGHT: Walls feature Farrow & Ball's "Skimming Stone" with water added and applied by Graham Menage to create a special effect.

RIGHT: The homeowners like to display painted French antiques in rooms where the sun threatens to fade natural wood, saying that painted furniture actually improves with sunlight.

Jean remembers the excitement of moving to France mixed with some dismay. When she first properly took in the shocking colors of the walls painted in greens, pinks, and chocolate browns, she says her heart sank. But before working out new color schemes, the structural problems had to be solved. Even 25 years in the property business in the UK had not quite prepared Doug. He admits, "We were alarmed when the structural engineer discovered the floors and ceilings were actually coming away from the rampart walls. From then on, the house became a building site. For 16 months, there was a concrete mixer sitting in the kitchen for most of the time, not to mention the layers of dust everywhere. We had to tie walls in with metal bars, and all floors and ceilings were rebuilt. The house was stripped to a shell."

The start of their antiques business was planned to be launched from a shop built into the cellars of the old house, and that, too, was a mammoth task to prepare. "We dug down 1.65 meters below ground and removed 150 tons of rubble to lay new foundations," Doug remembers. The one benefit of taking so long was the time they were able to spend researching materials for the house in a relaxed frame of mind. They scoured the district for reclaimed beams, tiles, and fireplaces to go with the style of the house, and Doug instructed his plasterers to produce "undulating, bumpy walls" to reflect its age.

Meanwhile, Jean produced color boards. "I always thought I would go with Provençal colors, rich blends of ochre and dusky terra-cotta, but in light of changing fashions, I have very recently cooled down my palette to white, blue, and grey. It is a plainer, paler, more restful look than the traditional way houses are decorated in the South of France. More recently, I have sold off big bookcases, rejigged the

A favorite Italian chandelier graces the dining room end of the kitchen. Green gingham curtains and painted furniture create a soft rural color scheme. The clock came off a church tower.

furniture, and radically decluttered. Lots of glass and china is now in storage. Being dealers, we are quite used to changing one piece for another. Though I have to admit, there are some pieces I get sentimental about but still try not to get too attached."

Jean's favorites are pale grey-blue painted 18th-century pieces, like the cupboard in the drawing room. Her style is romantic, rustic, and pared down mixed with plain voiles and checks. She loves to mix patterns and styles, but she is also a purist in that she will only display things she is passionate about, believing that "interiors knit together best when the elements are your own personal, passionate choice. They are bound to produce a coherence and harmony."

Doug indulged in his passion for buying paintings, and his second passion is people. "He loves to chat and deal with clients, which is why he was first to master the lingo," says Jean. But Doug has not forgotten his early linguistic gaffs. "I once told a client the table he wanted to buy was a solid 'dog' table, meaning solid oak. French for dog is 'chien,' of course, but 'chene,' which means oak, sounds so similar that it is easy to mix the two," he recalls. By now, Jean and Doug both speak fluent French and travel the world visiting antiques trade fairs in Dallas, New York, Palm Beach, and Battersea, a district of southwest London. In turn, a stream of foreign clients and friends repay visits to Mougins to stay in the Hills' romantic attic bedrooms overlooking the rooftops and lush undulating valleys below.

For the Hills, the fervor of their first love for France still remains constant. When they return from a foreign fair, they are struck by the magic of their French home and the views from the balcony that first won their hearts. In their attic office, they keep a huge comfortable sofa bed for afternoon naps. "Fortunately, the French take lunch breaks more seriously than most. Served with a glass or two of wine, most people still insist on an afternoon siesta. What more could one wish for?" asks Doug.

OPPOSITE: Sunlight filters though antique embroidered curtains in the kitchen, which was commissioned to incorporate a favorite cockerel motif fretted out of the cupboard doors. Cockerels are reflected in sconces and vases, too. The wall color is Farrow & Ball "Slipper Satin."

LEFT: Two new Velux skylights allow for a refreshing breeze to flow through the attic office on the top floor, which doubles as a sitting room. The blue painted French grandfather clock is a family favorite.

A wrought-iron antique bed hung with voile, combined with an 18th-century French chest of drawers, creates a light, romantic atmosphere in the master bedroom.

The top floor guest bedroom enjoys a view over Mougins' rooftops. The exposed timbered ceiling and beams are original. The bathroom on the top floor of the house has been decorated in traditional Delft tiles in blue and white, a favorite color combination in the South of France.

Movers
AND SHAKERS

Gloria and Eric Stewart restore houses in France,
mostly to live in themselves. They usually have
no intention of moving once a place is finished to
perfection, but then, suddenly, they are off again.
They find it almost impossible to pass up a fine
property in sad decline without wanting to put it back together
again. "We have been called serial movers," Gloria laughs, "but it
is never premeditated." Past moves have come about from looking
into estate agents' windows, but on the whole, they now avoid that
temptation. When they decided to move in 2006, they had no
particular property in view, but with their daughter and son grown
up and based in England, it was sensible to sell their large manor
in the Dordogne and find a property to restore of more manageable
size. This time, surely, it would be for the long term.

The Stewarts have lived in southwest France for more than
15 years, and they know the area well. Gloria had her own shop for a
time—trading covetable linens, antique furniture, and accessories—
in the pretty town of Trémolat, located on a bend of the Dordogne
River, and she still sells occasionally at textile fairs.

The farmhouse they found not far from their manor belonged to
an elderly couple who only used it for summer vacations, taking up
residence with their 15 grandchildren. Dating from around 1790,
the house was a single-story farmhouse with attic rooms. It had an

air of sophistication that made the Stewarts think it might possibly have been more than a farmhouse, perhaps a hunting lodge. "But the interior was very basic," Gloria says, "and there was no heating or reliable electrics. The owners went on a bit of a splurge in the 1970s, and there were horrible tiles on the floor and strange fabrics on the walls. They had taken out all the old doors and replaced them with typical factory-made ones." The location, however, was perfection. "It's not isolated, yet it feels as if it's in the middle of nowhere." Gloria adds. "From the terrace, there's an elevated view over treetops and, on the other side, fields of wildflowers and cultivated sunflowers." The Stewarts are masterly at sizing up a dispirited house and recognizing its underlying quality. There was a fireplace in the salon dating from the 18th century—so beautiful, and the design, so rare. The *pisé dent* floor in the kitchen, made from cobbles with pointed roots like teeth for hammering straight into the earth, was original. "Friends tried to warn us off, saying it was a dull house," Gloria says, "but we saw something that spoke to us. In the end, it was the location and the fireplace that decided us."

There was far too much work to be done for the Stewarts to live in the house while it was restored. They rented a small property nearby so that they could come on-site regularly to monitor progress. "The first job was to install a heating system," Gloria explains, "and we chose underfloor oil heating to avoid having to use radiators. It was an opportunity to take up all the modern tiles on the ground floor and replace them with reclaimed antique terra-cotta tiles local to the region."

Structural changes have been so seamlessly integrated that it's impossible to see that they have happened at all. "We changed the use of rooms on the ground floor so that what had been a bedroom, next to the salon, became the dining room. Then we made a new opening from the dining room into the salon with full-height bookshelves on each side of it. There was no proper hall, and the front door opened straight into the kitchen. We built a dividing wall to create a proper hallway and inserted an 18th-century partially glazed door to lead into the kitchen."

The original staircase came off the corner of the kitchen, so the Stewarts took that one out and built a staircase coming off the newly created hall. They installed 18th-century windows with their original latches on the turn of the stairs and above the kitchen sink. "We also replaced a horrible, cheap front door with a 17th-century door with its original fittings," Gloria adds. Walking into the re-ordered space, one wonders how it could ever have been different.

Understanding how to source and use architectural antiques is part of the Stewarts' skill. They found an 18th-century *cheminée de mariage* at an architectural salvage yard in Charente. "This style of fireplace would have been made by a local stonemason for the kitchen of a newly married couple," Gloria explains. "These fireplaces always have a heart carved in the stone somewhere. This *cheminée* fit perfectly into the kitchen, where previously there had been a huge hole in the wall with a wooden lintel. I love an open fire in the kitchen."

Upstairs, in what once would have been nothing more than attic space, were a run of five pokey little bedrooms and one small bathroom. The Stewarts re-ordered the space to create two bedrooms,

ABOVE: A modern front door was replaced with a 17th-century oak door, complete with its original forged iron fittings.

OPPOSITE: Reclaimed sets were laid in a decorative arrangement on the approach to the front door. The lucarne window above the door is said to represent Louis XIV, the Sun King, with the curved top symbolizing the sun and the curls, the hairs of his wig. Windows and shutters are painted in Farrow & Ball's "Light Blue."

Gloria designed the doors to the kitchen cupboards in latticework with wire behind. They are painted in "Sudbury Yellow" by Farrow & Ball. The 19th-century blue-and-white tiles behind the sink were a job lot Gloria found at a *brocante* sale.

OPPOSITE: A new hallway between the salon and the new stairs was created by building a wall to section off the kitchen. The hall furniture includes an 18th-century trumeau mirror incorporating a landscape scene, placed above an 18th-century painted console table with a marble top.

RIGHT: In the center of the spacious kitchen is a large table covered with a 19th-century patterned indigo-dyed cloth. Chairs are made from chestnut wood with woven backs, typical of this part of France. The fireside chair is covered in an early vintage tablecloth. Walls are in "Pointing;" beams in "Joa's White;" windows, doors, and cupboard tops in "Light Blue"—all Farrow & Ball. The fireplace, a *cheminée de mariage*, came from an architectural salvage company to provide a focus for the room.

each with its own bathroom. "We wanted to keep a feeling of open space up here," Gloria explains, "so instead of having a third bedroom suite, we have a big open landing." They were comfortable limiting the number of bedrooms because they converted a barn in the garden into a combination studio, office, and guest accommodation.

Color choice and furniture arrangement spring from Gloria's understanding of French and English style and how they can interact, particularly in the salon. "For us, a salon—or sitting room—has to be welcoming, restful, and cozy, which differs from the look of a classic French salon. The French sit upright on smart chairs rather than sinking into squashy, comfy sofas." Gloria's color choices often take reference from a fabric. In this house it's the salon curtains in a creamy linen from Chelsea Textiles, softly embroidered in tints of grey-blue and sand. The salon walls are lime-washed and colored with pigment to the warm white of the linen. It's a palette that runs through the house in related light neutrals, often with Farrow & Ball's "Light Blue" for woodwork. "I use 'Light Blue' a lot," Gloria says. "It's right for this part of France and has a wonderful quality of picking up the hues of other colors, changing sometimes to seem grey, sometimes green."

Many of the textiles she uses are antique, the cream of a collection she has gathered over the years. Antique quilts, curtains, pelmets, a monogrammed bedlinen and table linen, are mainly French, and pictures include her collection of much-loved 18th-century paintings and embroideries featuring baskets.

Once restored, the house was the perfect size for the Stewarts, and all the friends who had warned them not to buy have had to eat their words. "It feels happy now," Gloria observes. Whether that means they've settled for good remains an open question.

OPPOSITE: The wide windowsill in the dining room is a display area for a mercury candlestick, a marriage purse embroidered with doves and hearts, and a Parisian street scene painted in oils.

LEFT: The dining room tablecloth is made from an antique linen sheet, vegetable-dyed to a soft taupe color. The painted china cupboard is 19th-century Italian. The door beside the cupboard leads to a little office. Green glassware is made in the town of Biot in the South of France.

Comfortable sofas grouped around the fireplace are a typically English placement of furniture that works perfectly in a French setting. Sofas are covered in Linara by Romo, and cushions are in embroidered and check fabrics by Chelsea Textiles. The coffee table is an oak farmhouse table with its legs sawn off. The flooring features terra-cotta tiles overlaid with Oriental and berber rugs. Shelving along the wall between the salon and the dining room was built by a local carpenter.

CLOCKWISE FROM LEFT: Objects displayed on the salon windowsill include 18th-century boxes, a chinoiserie plate, and a miniature chest of drawers. A French Régence (1720–1740) chair with the top cover removed reveals calico on the seat and check fabric on the back. A 19th-century floral painting hangs above an English three-legged cricket table in the salon.

ABOVE: The kitchen door and the hall window are reclaimed 18th-century fittings. Walls are painted in "String" and woodwork in "Light Blue," both Farrow & Ball.

RIGHT: A reclaimed 18th-century window casts light over the new oak staircase that leads up from the hall. Paintings on the wall are by English artist, Fred Cuming RA.

LEFT: An oil painting of Flora hangs on rose-tinted limewashed walls in the second bedroom. Vintage undyed hemp sheets are overlaid with a pair of antique white Provencal quilts. The headboard framework is filled with pieces of 18th-century toile de Jouy. The bear is made from fragments of antique textile by Nathalie Pède.

OPPOSITE: Walls in the main bedroom are in limewash tinted with old rose pigment, suggested by the color in the bedcover made in fabric by Robert Kime.

Château
DE CHRISTIN

There's a word that adequately describes this little château nestling in the Languedoc countryside, and that is magical. From the wood paneling and intricate murals inside to the heady scent of the ancient rose bushes and medicinal garden outside, this is truly a haven of tranquility.

Nina and Oliver de la Fargue were living near Marseilles when they made the decision to move. "We'd had enough of living on the outskirts of the city in Marseilles. So rather than living in the suburbs, which was neither the city nor the countryside, we opted for a rural life and started to look for something suitable. We wanted a property right in the countryside, somewhere peaceful, but preferably near the coast," says Nina. "The Côte d'Azur was an obvious starting point, but it can be very touristy and extremely expensive. This area was a total contrast. It seemed to have everything—beautiful, quiet countryside with less expensive properties," she says.

As they weren't in any rush, the couple took their time to find the perfect property. "We looked for about a year," says Nina, "and in that time, we probably viewed about 12 potential properties. When we saw this place for the first time, we were completely stunned— we fell in love with it," Nina recalls.

The château was originally built in the 13th century as a second home and hunting lodge for the Marquis d'Aubais, a minor aristocrat, and his family. In 1792, during the French Revolution, the château was partly destroyed, although some of the original house, such as the Louis XIV balustrade and the Louis XVIII fireplaces are still intact today.

It was then restored by the De Baschi family. Originally Italian, they decided to give the place a Venetian flavor, which is instantly recognizable from the coronet on the top of the building.

Highly skilled craftsmen and artists carried out the meticulous renovation, which included wood paneling, flooring, and cabinetry, as well as the murals and trompe l'oeil painting, giving new life to the impressive family mansion.

The couple duly sold their business, which dealt with publishing instruction manuals, and bought the property, knowing that not only were they embarking on a big move to the country, they were also taking the house as a chambre d'hôte, or a luxury bed and breakfast.

Luckily, they could set up quickly. Although the original château was old, there was actually very little they had to do. "Everything was already in place," says Nina. "Pretty much all we had to do was bring our suitcases. The top two floors had been renovated, and all the murals and interior decoration had been done."

Much of the work was carried out by their friend and designer Richard Goullet, as well as Jean-Loup Daraux, the former being inspired by the natural world he saw around him. "The bedrooms in particular show his skill," says Nina. "Many of them have a theme, such as tulips or herbs, but my favorite is the bird bedroom. It's so light and airy, and I love the way Richard used nature, history, and trompe l'oeil to create an almost seamless link to the gardens below."

Downstairs, magnificent French family furniture graces the sitting room, dining room, and snug (similar to a den). Hundreds of fresh flowers and old roses from the garden mellow the opulence of each area, giving the whole place a sense of calm, personality, and unavoidable charm.

"I love flowers," admits Nina, "and even when we're eating outside, I love to decorate our dining table." In fact, Nina loves them so much, they are what she paints on her own hand-thrown pottery. "When I can, I sneak into our barn where I have a kiln and throw, paint, and glaze my pottery," she says. "I admit I would like to spend more time there, but with so many friends and people coming to stay, let alone the occasional wedding in our tiny garden chapel, it's difficult. Besides, sometimes it's so nice just to sit and enjoy the tranquility of our rural haven," she says.

OPPOSITE: The elegant, sweeping staircase is an original part of the property.

Richard Goullet used painting techniques around the traditional French fireplace that give the appearance of fine Italian marble.

OPPOSITE: The kitchen is where the family congregates for casual meals, while the door leads outside to a patio for alfresco dining.

Richard Goullet's trompe l'oeil handiwork can be seen on the walls of the dining room.

In the Herbalist room, the walls are painted in "Lichen," Estate Emulsion, from Farrow & Ball. The handy glass storage jars are from the Old English range from Divertimenti. Scalloped-edge bedding adds a feminine touch to this unusually delightful bedroom.

The Marquis bedroom features
hand-painted panels, a trumeau
mirror over the fireplace, and a
floor-to-ceiling antique wardrobe.
A hidden door near the bed in the
Marquis bedroom leads to the en
suite bathroom.

Nina de la Fargue's favorite bedroom is the bird room, due to its light and the lovely views. The trompe l'oiel on these walls are a mixture of paint effects and real pages taken from an old French book.

NEXT SPREAD: Even the outdoor dining table receives Nina's passion for flowers. Ancient roses line the path to the swimming pool, and surround the medicinal garden.

Champagne CHIC

Domaine de la Creuse is located in Champagne, the French district famous for the cultivation of the divine drink. It's also just a stone's throw away from the beautiful historic town of Troyes and the highway heading south. This makes the *chambre d'hôtes* a perfect stop for a night or two, but the wonderfully decorated guest rooms and suites will probably seduce you to linger a bit longer. Marie-Christine awaits you with *grand plaisir*.

Both Marie-Christine and Philippe Deroin-Thevenin are fond of meeting new people, and they liked the idea of starting a guesthouse. Philippe was born in the region, and Marie-Christine was born and raised in Provence, but she moved to the Champagne district 34 years ago when she and Philippe got married. "We used to live in a village nearby," Marie-Christine says. "Unfortunately, it developed into a small city. We love the countryside, so we decided that we wanted to move. Besides, we wanted to create a professional activity that we could share and to give Philippe a chance to slowly end his administrating career. I've always loved to welcome guests and to take good care of them. When I heard that Domaine de la Creuse was for sale, I knew our dream could become true."

Living in the area, Marie-Christine already knew the property. "I had been reading articles about it in interior magazines, and I had always been intrigued by it," she says. "I even visited it several times just out of curiosity. When we went to have a look as prospective buyers, I felt like I was stepping into a fairy tale. It was so gorgeous! I simply adored the lovely old roses that were covering the façades and the marvellous architectural features, like the 18th-century half-timbered walls of the house and the 19th-century brick stone walls of the outbuildings." The couple is head over heels to have found their new home.

The farmhouse was originally built in the 18th century, and some of the outbuildings were added in the 19th century. In the old days, Domaine de la Creuse served as a farm for the owners of a castle, Château de Villebertin. When Marie-Christine and Philippe purchased the house, it was in quite good condition, thanks to the previous owners. "They did a tremendous job renovating the place, carefully preserving the architectural characteristics, the plan, and the soul of the farmer's origin," Marie-Christine says. "Besides restoring the buildings, they created the five guest rooms. They loved to travel and were passionate about finding and using old building materials, which they hunted for in flea markets and in antiques stops. Over the years they had collected many old doors, shutters, sinks, and furniture, which they had kept in storage. But those items finally found a wonderful second life on this domain."

The five guest rooms and suites are located in the farm's outbuildings, and each has its own name. *Pivoine* (peony) is the old *battoir à blé*, where grain was once threshed. *Seringat* (jasmine) and *Bergerie* are located in a former *bergerie*—an old sheepfold, *Ãscot* is a former stable, and *Muscari* is in the old henhouse. In each of the guest quarters, one can discover traces of its origin, such as original beams, clay and brick walls, and the old cratches in guest rooms *Bergerie* and *Ãscot*—all beautiful remnants of a past long gone. In no other means do the rooms resemble their former function. Once sturdy, bare, and basic, they now exude a romanticism, a style that Marie-Christine calls *Campagne Chic* (Country Chic). Each room has its own character, achieved in part by the use of carefully chosen color schemes, such as Scandinavian gray and blue in *Muscari*, cheerful red in *Pivoine*, stylish taupe and ivory in *Bergerie*, and honey, sand, and café au lait hues in *Seringat*. Beautiful textiles—like curtains, bed linens, and upholstery in checks, stripes, and toile de Jouy—combined with antique fabrics complete the personal look of each room.

Marie-Christine has a passionate interest in interior decoration. She was lucky and privileged to find this historical home and these wonderful guest rooms that were already decorated by the previous owners. "She sewed all the curtains and new upholstery by hand," she says. "Philippe and I wanted to add even more comfort and update some things to contemporary standards, such as adding flat-screen televisions. But we wanted to accomplish this without disturbing the warm, soft, and stylish

ABOVE: Heartbreaker Mezzo is a Lagotto Romagnolo, so he's always keen to play! This affectionate dog is also a smart hunter for *truffes* (truffles), a dainty and otherwise pricey delicacy served with your breakfast eggs.

OPPOSITE: A variety of cozy seating areas outdoors allows for relaxation and private conversation. As weather allows, guests may enjoy breakfast under a canopy of gently rustling leaves. Fresh table linens add a sense of occasion to any gathering, as do flowers picked from the garden for a centerpiece.

ABOVE: All the antique furniture and accessories come from family members of Marie-Christine and Philippe, including the silverware, crockery, and table linens. Older pieces are used alongside new crockery.

OPPOSITE: The couple stores crockery and vintage serving pieces, including those made of porcelain and silver, in an old medical cabinet.

atmosphere—an atmosphere that one finds in a family home, a place to spend time together, to relax and to be happy."

Apart from enjoying the beautiful rooms, guests will also find lots of relaxation in the garden, created on the *cour central*, the central courtyard. Several seating options allow everyone to linger in privacy, listening to the sound of whispering leaves in the old chestnut trees. When a bit chilly, one can walk to a lovely decorated garden room, created in a building that once stored the farm's machinery.

An early highlight of the day is breakfast, prepared with delicious homemade ingredients, like jams and chutneys, and served by Marie-Christine in the garden or in the breakfast room. "This room is entirely decorated with our own family antiques," she says. "We love the idea of giving them a second life by having them in this room. They all serve as a theatrical background for breakfast! I like it very much that beautiful, old, everyday objects are now seen and used again—silver napkin rings, salt shakers, crockery, glassware, table linens—objects that have been used and cherished by many generations and are still used by us and our guests."

LEFT: The daybed in the children's bedroom is decorated with joyful blue-and-white checks to complement the Scandinavian color scheme.

OPPOSITE, LEFT: The rod windows near this cozy seating area feature fabulous textiles. The previous homeowner handmade the curtains. The fauteuils (armchairs with open sides and upholstered arms) were re-upholstered with matching fabric.

OPPOSITE, RIGHT: To achieve a relaxing aesthetic in *Muscari*, the owners used shades of grays and blues—softer hues often associated with Scandinavian style—in the guest room, adjacent bathroom, and for the old beams. The bathtub is new.

Combining the gentle hues of of honey, sand, and café au lait with soft materials guarantees an ultra-comfortable stay in *Seringat*, a former sheepfold.

OPPOSITE, CLOCKWISE FROM ABOVE LEFT: The owners discovered the wooden mantel piece at a *brocante*. This niche houses old books, a framed piece of handmade embroidery, and an old photo showing a family member of the previous owners. Robust, large pieces of *dalle de pierre* (stone slabs) function as washbasin furniture in *Seringat*. The curtain was handmade using old textiles. Lovely, old garments now serve as a romantic decoration.

DANIEL PENNAC

MERCI

nrf

OPPOSITE: *Pivoine* exudes utter romance, from the canopy bed to lovely textiles mixed and matched in a variety of red-and-white patterns. Old shutters now serve as wardrobe doors.

BELOW: The small sofa and chairs were re-upholstered with matching fabric. The former homeowner stitched the framed embroidery work. The curtains were handmade by the former owner of the house.

Ãscot was formerly a stable. The original manger can still be seen in the entry. The old horse-riding boots came from a great-uncle of Philippe; the other equipment was already there. The bedlinens are new.

In olden days, a farmer stored his machinery in this outbuilding. Now it's a cozy place to linger in the garden when it's too hot or a bit rainy outside.

Vintage
PASSION

"I believe whole-heartedly that every house has a different personality," says Donna, who for 10 years tinkered and tweaked her French country abode. "Don't try to pull it all together at once. It's gratifying to take the time to putter until one day you step back and say, 'There, that's what she was trying to convey.'"

And for this particular sun-splashed stucco space, the lesson was in essentials. The day after Donna closed on her home, she stripped it of its kitchen cabinets, solid countertops, and built-in bookshelves, granting herself the freedom to make such swaps as a vintage French wine rack for dish storage and a paint-stripped farm table for a prep surface. "It's amazing what a little confidence can carry off," Donna promises. "Decide what works for you, and don't look back."

Donna's confidence, to be sure, is bolstered by her lifelong passion for collecting vintage treasures. Owner of The Gray Door, a premier antiques shop in Houston, Texas, Donna surrounds herself with fabulous finds from across the globe. "I don't buy inventory unless I would live with it," she says. And what she chooses to live with is an eclectic survey of largely French, English, and Italian furnishings.

Formal 18th- and 19th-century pieces are balanced by easy-care fabrics and quirky accent pieces, creating a welcoming setting for entertaining. Dining and living rooms have been swapped back and

LEFT: Donna's book collection includes the twine-tied history of the French Revolution and a set of vellum English translations of 19th-century Giorgio Vasari works. Coral and shells are another beloved collector's item that remind Donna of her childhood summers spent in the Bahamas.

forth to suit both whim and occasion, while the kitchen's easy transition to a comfortable seating area opens up the smaller-size floor plan.

Without traditional countertops and cabinetry, the simplified kitchen hosts only everyday necessities. Dishware, glasses, a microwave, and mixing bowls make their home on a vintage metal wine cabinet, while frequently used appliances can tuck away in an English baker's counter. Anchoring the space and housing the sink and dishwasher in style is a one-of-a-kind island crafted from a French shop counter, known as a comptoir.

Yet the cleverest choice Donna said she made in the home was inspired by another designer, John Saladino, who commonly uses drapery to distinguish rooms. Bothered by her home's lack of a foyer and the obtrusiveness of the staircase, she decided to hang a sheer panel to create a comfortable niche. Equal parts linen, silk, and wool, the curtain is now a brilliant backdrop that still allows in light from a second-story skylight.

"It was fun to give myself total permission not to be practical," Donna recalls of her years living in this friend of a home. "It will always be freeing to set aside tradition and surround yourself with only the things that make you happy."

LEFT: To balance the formality of a 17th-century Flemish tapestry, Donna selected a slipcovered Saladino sofa, a French bergère, a tea table, and a footrest. "I love 17th- and 18th-century antiques, but I'm not a snob about it," Donna says. "Items like footrests, benches, and garden tables are flexible and un-stuffy. It's important that people feel relaxed and comfortable in my home."

BELOW: In the place of built-in bookcases that once flanked the living room fireplace, Donna created an alcove with tall weathered shutters, a stately French server, an Italian chest, and Italian confit jars.

LEFT: Stripped of its bright pink paint, this old farm table with a layer of European tiles replaces a traditional countertop, while an upside-down pastry counter shelf displays serving items.

OPPOSITE: Connecting the kitchen to the sitting area, a 10-foot English baker's counter packs plenty of storage options for kitchen and dining needs.

OPPOSITE: One of the homeowner's most signature design choices was her selection of an 18th-century French shop counter, which was retrofitted to hold her dishwasher and sink.

LEFT: A vintage metal wine cabinet is a hutch for Donna's dishes. She removed two-thirds of the wine racks and replaced them with sheets of stainless steel for supportive shelves.

RIGHT: This hardworking office space features a Louis XVI-style desk and Parisian library shelves packed with market baskets.

OPPOSITE: This entrance courtyard's driftwood bench, folding bistro chairs, French tiles, cistern planter, and pear trees set a European scene for morning coffee or an evening cocktail.

OPPOSITE: The master bedroom's 19th-century English iron and walnut campaign bed was once used in an ornate general's tent. Donna chose linen for the skirt and back hanging, while hand-woven antique French sheets layer the rest of the bed.

RIGHT: Donna's favorite niche features an 18th-century Louis XVI settee, Swedish bergère, and old artwork, including an 18th-century sketch of the Madonna and two floral copperplate engravings.

Lovely LEGACY

Julianne Hanna loves a warm but simply elegant style, and after locating their charming abode, she and husband Kevin began to enhance the existing architecture and interiors. The couple, along with their two daughters, adore the setting of the home near a golf course and small lake, which provides a suburban feel and quiet ambiance for their family.

The soft color palette of the living room with its coffered ceiling, warm-colored bricked fireplace, and antique crystal chandelier make a relaxed, yet elegant backdrop for unique furnishings that bring the style to life. Statement drapery adds a bit of frivolity to this lovely setting, where they, too, welcome guests. The same colors are repeated throughout the living area, unifying the style in the home.

The dining room is reminiscent of a French cottage, with embroidered chair slipcovers alongside the antique dining table. A large chicken-wired cabinet mixes practical but bucolic storage with a formal look. The leaning vertical mirror makes a dramatic stance along one wall, with a rustic French column tastefully used as a plant podium.

ABOVE: "Open and spacious, with treasures from travels abroad," says Julianne Hanna of her home décor, as she cannot resist displaying special pieces found and collected. Textiles are especially beautiful, such as the needlepoint pillows and a cherished family Bible. Terrazzo tile floors add an earthy tone and are used throughout the main level of the home.

The spacious kitchen and cook area provide a welcoming flow. The family truly uses this area as the gathering place to share family time. In the adjoining sitting room, the fireplace has an arrangement of club chairs. The garden views make this room everyone's favorite. The circular setting allows for easy conversation and time spent together after dinner. Quartzite countertops, hand selected, add a soft caramel look, while a matte-finish bookcase, custom pantry doors, and cabinetry add the fine details to the sunny room. The kitchen is organized to store away clutter, making it open for entertaining anytime.

From the small library in the front of the house, the peaceful bedrooms, and powder rooms, to the old bench welcoming guests outside, this home is gracious and inviting—just like the family that dwells inside.

PREVIOUS PAGES: Travertine tile floors in the kitchen and dining spaces give a warm French country feel and complement these rooms for entertaining. A mix of wood finishes and small cabinet units add light to the rooms, as do mirrored tiles that surround each side of the pass-through to the living room. The antique bookshelf has a variegated greenish-gray hue to draw the eye toward small fine artwork pieces and collectible pottery. Sliding doors designed for ease of use cleverly hide the pantry storage closet.

LEFT: High-back end chairs and monogrammed slipcovers on side chairs surround the dining table. Open windows are graced only by soft green panels, while a leaning vertical mirror reflects natural light from the opposite wall.

The master bedroom is soft and poetic with the simplicity of shades of white. Fabric with touches of gold covers the salon chair, and a swath of cream lace adds to the dappled light play from window linens.

LEFT: A puddled bed skirt is topped with a playful floral slipcover and pillow, while a rustic headboard crowns the bed. A tiny vertical row of mirrors embellishes the wall.

BELOW: A French cabinet was transformed into the vanity for a guest bath, with a charming tiled backsplash above and copper wash accessories below.

RIGHT: The twig-inspired flea market bench holds cuttings from the day's garden finds.

French
COUP DE COEUR

A s an exchange student, Mary Stuart McCamy fell in love with the Dordogne and Lot River Valleys nestled within the resplendent Périgord region of southwestern France. The warm and welcoming people, the stunning landscapes, the impossibly charming villages, and the area's rich history and ancient pilgrimage routes have lured her back countless times ever since. Having explored the valleys slowly over the years on both foot and bicycle—with the climate, food, and wine an added bonus—she continues to discover a new *coup de coeur* with every bend in the river.

"Thirty years ago, I vowed I would live in a *Périgourdine* house one day," says Mary Stuart, a Washington, D.C., literacy tutor who also, as it turns out, has an innate talent for interior decorating. "Actually, I wanted to live in a *pigeonnier*—after cleaning it thoroughly—but in the end, that seemed impractical with four children," she laughs. "So, I asked Ankie Barnes if he could design a new traditional home that would incorporate some of my favorite architectural elements from the region," she says.

Having spent a great deal of time in the French countryside himself, Washington, D.C., architect Anthony "Ankie" Barnes needed no explanation when Mary Stuart proposed a design wish list that included snubbed gables, a *pigeonnier* (dovecote), quoins, stone sills, a cobbled courtyard, rough-sawn posts and lintels, reclaimed ceiling beams complete with adze marks, and rounded wall corners inside and out. They also had the great fortune of finding a lot that backed up to sprawling parkland on two sides, an ideal setting for a home designed in the rural vernacular. To make the residence look more like a French country farmhouse rather than a townhouse in the city, Ankie scaled down the front profile of the home and added rustic elements to keep the style informal. The foyer and stair landing were designed to echo the farmhouses of France, which are often organized around a central courtyard and reclaimed outdoor spaces once used to shelter grain and animals. To ensure visual continuity, these quaint areas also feature the same tumbled limestone bricks that were used to cobble the entry courtyard. Squared off with a hipped roof, flared eaves, and quoins, a stair tower anchoring the two wings of the house nods to the picturesque dovecotes of the Périgord region and also creates an asymmetrical roofline that adds to the informality of the home's front elevation.

Out back, the lot tumbles down to a spring-fed creek—not exactly the Dordogne River Valley with villages built right into the slopes, but it presented an opportunity to create a more terraced elevation that takes advantage of the natural landscape. A completely above-ground lower level with multiple sets of French doors leads to a shaded loggia that offers a cool respite for the hot D.C. summers.

"This is the children's favorite relaxation spot," says Mary. "Mine is the terrace above that looks out over the surrounding parkland. The landscaping was as important as the home design," she adds, "and we had the privilege of working on the garden design with landscape architects Leslie Gignoux and Scott Fritz, another team of remarkably talented Francophiles."

Leslie and Scott found the perfect balance between structured garden spaces and looser transitional zones where the yard meets the surrounding woods. The stonework they designed is especially stunning and reminiscent of the building materials in southwestern France. Their custom blend of stones for the walls, piers, and chimneys in a serene palette of buff, rust, cream, and sienna brown complements the home's stucco exterior, as well as the lighter shades of the paving material.

"My family was involved in every step of the design process, from wandering around stone quarries to visiting old barns to select beams," says Mary. "We wanted to incorporate as many reclaimed, heavily textured, and organic materials as possible—the more imperfect the better," she adds.

Throughout her entire house, rustic and weathered materials bring layers of texture and timeless patina to the overall design scheme. Lustrous wood floors in random widths and lengths are made of reclaimed antique oak, and old ceiling beams are split, hacked, twisted, and discolored. The courtyard and foyer pavers are tumbled and irregular, and many of the antique light fixtures take on the wonderfully heavy tarnishing of age. Even the paint and wall treatments were mottled and brushed to replicate a distressed look with variations in the finish.

"We decided all this imperfection makes us feel more comfortable," says Mary, "and it seems to have that effect on our guests as well," she laughs. "We relied on Ankie to advise us on proportions and details, including casement window styles and authentic ceiling beam patterns, and we also

OPPOSITE: Striking architectural features, including a magnificent stone fireplace, rustic ceiling beams, and soaring French doors and windows, give the family room an airy and spacious feel. Homeowner Mary Stuart McCamy kept the décor intentionally simple and chose colors that echoed the neutral palette of the fireplace. Rusty and crusty light fixtures, an elegant seagrass rug, and a side table made of petrified wood bring gorgeous texture and patina to this inviting living space.

The kitchen was designed around a mid-19th-century butcher block from the Périgord region. "I wanted the look of a more unfitted kitchen that was still functional for a large family blessed with lots of visitors," says Mary Stuart. The kitchen cabinets and open shelving were created by Heartwood Design, as was the cabinetry in the adjoining library and dining room. The graceful gothic arches in the kitchen are reiterated in the fireplace surround and elsewhere throughout the house.

consulted with friends Elizabeth Boland and Caroline Wilson, the mother-daughter team behind Design in a Day, who were especially helpful with lighting selections and pulling together stray antiques in a way that made sense," she adds.

A favorite space for gathering with friends and family, Mary's inviting kitchen is centered around a mid-19th-century *billot* (butcher block) from the Périgord region. The room's elegant gothic arches are repeated in the fireplace surround and elsewhere in the home. Throughout this extraordinary dwelling, many of the sconces are made from repurposed architectural elements, and the floor coverings are all natural, neutral, and highly textured. Quiet and serene, the interior color palette is mostly pale and muted with the exception of the light blue-green of the windows and doors that frame the surrounding landscape during the day and add a subtle splash of color at night.

"It has been an absolute joy to live and raise my children in this home," says Mary. "It is a cozy family house most of the time but can graciously accommodate groups of friends and larger celebrations. The informal design and indoor-outdoor flow make it an easy place to gather," she adds. "In fact, we don't considerate it a successful weekend unless we find a couple of stowaway guests in the basement or loft."

Rustic
FRENCH ALLURE

With an astute eye for the authentic, Ruth Gay intentionally designed her Houston, Texas, home to embody the distinctive look and feel of a French *bastide*. Those who know her would expect no less from this founder and owner of Château Domingue, one of the country's premier importers of reclaimed and aged architectural elements and monumental antiques. Fueled by a deep appreciation and passion for Old-World history and architecture, Ruth has journeyed to Europe countless times and scoured many roads off the beaten path to unearth her amazing cache of rare and exceptional antiques.

"I am drawn to authentic materials with warmth and charm, so the South of France is always an inspiration to me," says Ruth. "When I saw *La Bastide de Marie* in *Ménerbes*, I knew I wanted something similar in atmosphere—rooms that are informal, yet still refined," she adds. "Even though the architecture is all stone and history is all around you, there's a glow and a lightness, a very welcoming vibe."

Working closely with Houston interior designer Pamela Pierce, the owner of Pierce Designs & Associates and also the creator of an overwhelmingly popular French-inspired blog called *Cote de Texas*, Ruth followed her own personal taste for materials in their natural state—stone, wood, wrought iron, and terra-cotta—nothing

PREVIOUS PAGES: From the inviting entrance hall, rustic yet elegant limestone definitely sets the stage for the tone and palette of the stone-lined gallery and dining room. Antique *bugets*—building blocks of limestone—form the walls in the gallery, and floors of Bars de Montpellier run throughout the ground floor.

The two large urns flanking the front steps are antique terra-cotta vases d'Anduze. Two rival families were known for making these urns that were most often used as vessels for orange trees in château gardens.

OPPOSITE: Pan-European furnishings in the sitting room include chairs from France, a pair of Italian mirrors, and a Swedish tea table topped with Delft tiles. These otherwise disparate pieces are beautifully united by their 18th-century provenance and soft palette.

LEFT: Pieces of 16th-century Valencian lusterware that the homeowner collected one by one are arranged on top of an Italian console table from the 18th century. "I love the colors and subtle glow of the ceramic pieces and the exuberance of the cartouches on the apron of the table," says Ruth.

too glossy or glitzy. Throughout her home, an array of colorful hand-painted Delft tiles and cherished collectibles, including Valencian lusterware and exceptional blue-and-white faience pieces illustrate her preferred aesthetic. A vaulted ceiling in the study made of limestone *bugets* surprisingly gives the room an uplifting feel without being heavy, and reclaimed wood ceilings bring warmth and coziness to the breakfast room. A well-curated mix of Old-World antiques from France, Sweden, and Italy sit side by side harmoniously, united by their gracefully weathered patinas and soft color palettes. Crisp linen fabrics and dressed-down slipcovered furniture sprinkled throughout create a comfortable and relaxed atmosphere in most every room in the house.

"I love that there is a casual, comfortable feel everywhere in my home," says Ruth. "We entertain a lot, and the house very easily accommodates big groups of people while still feeling intimate because there are numerous rooms to gather in," she notes.

The kitchen is undoubtedly Ruth's favorite space in her home, and like most houses, the place where everyone seems to always end up. Outfitted almost entirely in stone and wood, the room exudes a rustic and welcoming atmosphere, with nearly every piece telling a story. A charming stone sink and stone countertops—both salvaged from an 18th-century monastery in the South of France—bring elegant aged patina and a sense of Old-World beauty to this warmly inviting gathering spot. A convivial antique baker's table serves as the kitchen island, and people gravitate to it like they do to an open fire.

"I think timeless materials never go out of style," says Ruth. "If you want a room or a home to feel grounded—to have longevity, to feel real—then you have to use real things."

LEFT: A reclaimed wood ceiling, as well as a trumeau *cheminée*, bring warmth and charm to the breakfast room. A collection of blue-and-white faience sits atop a Swedish table and a sideboard, and the large vessel to the left of the fireplace—called a *biot*—was traditionally used for preserving olives.

LEFT: Beautiful in their similarities as well as their subtle differences, these apothecary jars that were collected over time make a stunning display.

OPPOSITE: "I find a big harvest table flanked by upholstered benches to be more inviting and convivial than a more formal table and chairs," says Ruth. "Guests feel relaxed and free to move about, trade places, and help themselves to seconds," she adds.

OPPOSITE: "My kitchen is furnished almost entirely with stone and wood," says Ruth. "The deep apron of the wooden island indicates that it was once a baker's table with large built-in bins for flour," she adds.

LEFT: A warm and inviting breakfast room features decidedly casual open shelving. "I like the informality of people being able to help themselves to plates, utensils, and napkins and then sit where they like," says Ruth.

LEFT: One of the homeowner's favorite pieces, a shallow stone sink in the kitchen, came out of an 18th-century monastery in the South of France. "The monks have a tradition of making and selling goat cheese," says Ruth, "so this sink was used for centuries up until very recently when it was replaced by a stainless steel one—lucky me," she laughs.

OPPOSITE: The vaulted ceiling in the study is made of limestone *bugets*. The antique lantern once lit the front of a stable, and the glass-paned doors enclosing the library shelves were formerly French windows.

Attention TO DETAIL

S tepping through doors adorned with custom wrought-iron designs and into an oval foyer, you know immediately that Teresa and Allen Hughes' home was built with care. Bursts of orange found in the French settee and the display of porcelain urns greet guests with a certain flair—the first of many very intentional decisions by Gretchen Edwards of Gilstrap Edwards Interior Design in Atlanta, Georgia. "Because the walls are neutral and most of the palette throughout the house is subtle, obviously we wanted the foyer to be a focal point," Gretchen notes.

The rest of the home exhibits a graceful, French country-inspired charm that takes its cues from the living room, where Gretchen used a combination of patterns and textures to add interest to the neutral palette. "I'd say the driving force for this particular room is the woven floral linen fabric that the curtains are made of," she says. The floral design is balanced by the geometric lines in the striped and checked upholstery, and Gretchen added pieces like the round light fixtures to create a play on shapes.

In the kitchen, furniture-like upper cabinets are hung on a backsplash of handmade tile. "It's a gorgeous, subtle, tone-on-tone geometric," Gretchen notes of the tile choice. "It's not a tile they'll tire of as easily or as quickly as something much more patterned." Continuing the theme of mixing textures and elements, the wooden

Striped silk curtains hung high on the wall infuse the dining room with a touch of color. An ornate chandelier dripping with crystal creates a focal piece over the dining set, and framed intaglios over the bar cart are an artistic touch.

island and upper cabinets were stained dark, creating a contrast with the softer, more refined elements of the tile and embroidered window dressings.

Gretchen accomplished her goal for the master bedroom—to create a serene, calming retreat—via a creamy color palette and subtle, carefully selected patterns. A padded fabric, which adds detail to the walls, has the bonus effect of softening noise within the space. The carpet features an understated damask pattern. "The sheer curtains add a softness, of course," Gretchen notes, "but the floral pattern that was used for the curtains and bed shams picks up colors all the way from the living room and dining room and helps with the flow throughout the house."

The en suite bath utilizes marble floors and mirrored surfaces to add interest to a space washed in white and gray tones. "Just having that beautiful freestanding tub nestled in the oval space is fabulous," Gretchen says. "And I absolutely love the detail of the vanity table and the recessed glass shelves on each side of that."

Because wine-tasting is a passion for the homeowners, the wine cellar received the same careful attention given to the rest of the home. "Teresa wanted comfortable chairs to sit with friends for tasting, and those chairs are comfortable enough to sit for hours," Gretchen says of the monogrammed seating choices. Custom-made steel doors complement the stone floor and walls, and the wooden beams add yet another layer of texture to the space. Touches like these support Gretchen's assertion that "So much of interior design and what makes it successful…is the attention to detail."

The chairs in the breakfast area
are dressed in checked slipcovers
that speak elegance to French
country style. "I love the attention
to detail—it's more like dressmaker
details with the button closure on
the back and the banding on the
bias," Gretchen says.

A marble-topped accent table flanked by striped chairs features distressed wood carving. The collections showcased on top include mercury glass pieces and a lamp that Gretchen calls "a work of art in itself."

A powder blue stool across from an elegantly detailed mirror provides a comfortable place to get ready in the morning. The surface of the vanity reflects fresh-cut tulips, and a simple tray keeps everything tidy.

Wallpaper made to look like wine crates lines one wall of the cellar, a favorite touch of the designer. A table that Allen crafted from white oak sourced on the property holds the homeowners' latest tasting selection.

Signature STYLE

When the wind blows just so on a mild Texas morning, Yvette and Tim Leihgeber can smell a hint of fresh caramelized coffee through their cranked-open kitchen window. From a roaster just a few miles away, the warm aroma drifts onto their property, dancing through their grove of olive trees before tickling the lush herb garden just outside the heart of the Leihgebers' home.

This marriage of earth and dwelling, of scent and structure, is most certainly by design. "Every element of this house was intended to reflect our deep love of travel, especially our time in France," says Yvette, "and you can't reflect Paris without integrating all of the senses."

Built nearly nine years ago in Tyler, Texas, the home, modeled after a French château, features a beautiful blend of neoclassic, deco, contemporary, and French country style. Inside grand double doors, a French dot pattern among honed slate and travertine seems straight from a Parisian palace, setting the tone for a formal, yet inviting, ambiance.

Yvette, a self-taught fine artist and jewelry designer, crafted many features of the home herself, from draperies and pillows to layers of Annie Sloan chalk paint. Set against crisp white walls, much of the art is Yvette's as well, including female figure paintings and large-scale photography taken on family travels. Furnishings are gleaned

PREVIOUS PAGES AND ABOVE:
A grand sampler of the home's
eclectic style, the foyer features
a French market table and chairs,
terra-cotta olive jars, antique
columns, and chunky baskets.

from a lifetime of collecting, some from shops in Seaside, Florida, and others from antiques stores and European adventures.

Off the foyer, Tim's study is a masterful example of merging eras and styles. "I wanted this to feel like a Parisian apartment," she says, referring to details like a chunky basket-turned-table featuring iron details, white oak floors in a herringbone pattern, soaring cabinets, a honed black marble fireplace, and a hidden door that can close off the entire master suite.

In the couple's oldest daughter's room, chair rail-height blue-and-white faux finish adds an aged, mural-like patina, while features like roped handles on the nightstands and layers of neutral bed linens draw the eye to texture. "I do a lot of finishes on the furniture myself, and I love to leave it a bit rough around the edges," says Yvette of the distinct French country customization.

In another daughter's eclectic "Tiffany Room," white oak floors and chunky baskets balance timeless iron lamps, a neoclassic chest, and an antique mirror that was, as the homeowner proclaims, "rescued" from a thrift shop.

Frequent entertainers, the Leihgebers desired an easy-flow dining room overlooking the front gravel drive court. Leaning toward French modern, the room features shell chandeliers, slipcovered chairs, Versailles-pattern flooring, a Biedermeier table, a sky-high cityscape, and delicate linen drapes.

Back in the kitchen is a beautiful blend of different surfaces. A luxuriously large marble backsplash connects soapstone countertops to open shelving that was selected "before it was the trend." A marble island with stainless steel sides anchors the room, and a butcher block cart is ideal for prep work. In the adjacent breakfast area, a grand coconut-sliver chandelier is the focal point of the room.

"We dreamed and dreamed about this home and how it would serve our family," Yvette says. "What came to be was even more magnificent than we'd imagined." And with her hand in every detail—from the particularly placed palm fronds to the whitewashed wood—the home is most certainly hers, most certainly theirs, most certainly signature.

Steps from the foyer, this off-the-master study is reminiscent of a French apartment. Custom drapes and pillows, plus a duo of lamps and side tables, add delightful symmetry that also highlights original art by the homeowner.

PREVIOUS PAGES: Guests delight in dining among this room's statement pieces: a duo of abalone shell chandeliers, an antique French mirror, a small Biedermeier table, and Yvette's original art.

RIGHT: With the kitchen window cranked wide open, the homeowners can enjoy a fire pit, topiaries, and a variety of ready-to-savor herbs. Flanking the window are original photography canvases.

BELOW: A simple pot hanging system organizes oft-used kitchen wares in a stylish fashion.

The breakfast room is a balance of styles, from a more modern coconut chandelier to heirloom pieces like an antique pine bench and china cabinet. Selections from Yvette's fashionable hat collection become whimsical accents when displayed throughout the home.

PREVIOUS PAGES: Daughter Lauren's bedroom features a distinctive marble-like faux finish that adds a fresh color background to the room's otherwise neutral furnishings.

In the serene guest suite, a French armoire sits opposite a painted antique bed and game table. "If your finishes aren't exactly what you want, don't hesitate to change them," says Yvette. "I've pretty much chalk-painted in every room."

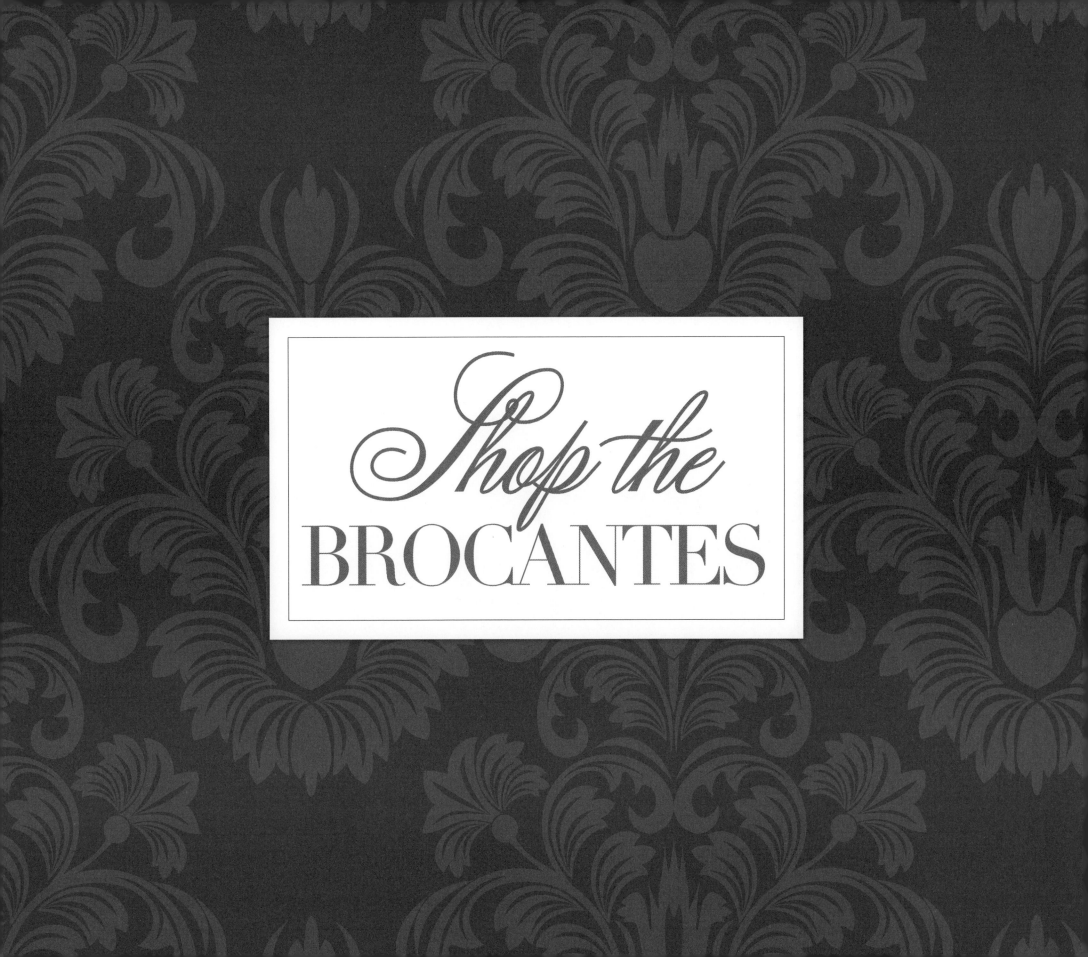

Shop the
BROCANTES

Treasures & ANTIQUES

France is a veritable paradise of Old-World antiques and fine vintage collectibles, and Provence is perhaps one of the most revered destinations in the country in which to shop these covetable wares. Nestled between the Mediterranean Sea and the picturesque region of Provence-Alpes-Côte d'Azur, this sun-drenched dreamlike setting offers endless unspoiled landscapes of rolling hills dotted with lush pines, charming wineries and villages, and, of course, the legendary flea markets, or *brocantes*, as they are known by the French.

Exploring these alluring open-air markets has become a captivating pastime and an idyllic way to spend an afternoon—or an entire weekend. Considered by some to deliver the kind of blissful ambience that the South of France is famous for, the charismatic flea markets pave the way for locals and visitors alike to enjoyably explore the quaint hidden alleys, delightful cobblestone streets, and meandering pathways that can be discovered throughout this enchanting destination.

The Brocante de Villeneuve-lès-Avignon is arguably one of the best flea markets in southern France. Situated against a stunning backdrop of a medieval city more than 700 years old, this once-a-week market features nearly a hundred professional exhibitors who gather along the ancient walls of the Fort St. André to sell their impressive array of antique furniture, fine china, crystal, glassware, vintage pottery, ceramics, sterling silver, wine-making implements, splendid kitchenware, and other rare collectibles. This celebrated market

attracts both flea market enthusiasts, who simply come to browse, and serious antiques dealers who come to snap up the best items during the wee morning hours.

Located just a few miles east of Avignon, the charming little village of L'Isle-sur-la-Sorgue is a mecca of antiques dealers and secondhand shops, and over the past 30 years, has become the capital city of antiques. Shopping is superb all year long, but major spring and summer antiques fairs boast 450 exhibitors and 120,000 visitors who flock to this quaint settlement to find the very best collectibles and memorabilia from the south of France.

For those looking to immerse themselves in the unique beauty and joie de vivre of an artistically rich and historic French village, a visit to St. Paul de Vence should definitely be on your list. A stroll through the ancient and winding roads of this locale reveals a multitude of shops featuring fine art, exceptional antiques, and one-of-a-kind collectibles. For some of the finest perfumes and handmade soaps in the region, a stop at the legendary Maison Godet is a definite must.

Quickly seduced by the exhilarating thrill of the hunt, shoppers new to the markets should make a note to always bring cash, as some dealers do not accept any other form of tender. Also, as haggling is typically appropriate at most venues, buyers need not be afraid to politely negotiate the best bargain with vendors. However, some of them will be more cooperative toward the end of the day, as they grow anxious to pack up. But no matter which flea market you choose to explore, a visit to any one of these captivating *brocantes* is in many ways its own reward. Happy hunting.

THIS PAGE: An antique French side table paired with a decidedly shabby chic wicker chair and a basket brimming with vintage linens sits in artful composure outside one of many quaint shops that line the streets of the legendary marketplace known as Villeneuve-lès-Avignon. Old glass jars holding a mishmash of quirky curiosities create an imaginative display.

OPPOSITE: Eye-catching vignettes of antiques, collectibles, and obscurities are undeniably part of the allure of shopping the outdoor flea markets and quaint shops that line the villages of southern France. Browsers can while away an entire day picking through an irresistible hodgepodge of antique hardware, vintage ephemera, and household odds and ends.

Maison Godet, the legendary and timeless perfume shop founded by Julien-Joseph Godet in Paris more than a hundred years ago, should definitely be on your must-see list of venues while browsing the enchanting streets of Saint Paul de Vence. Visitors are immediately drawn in by the stunning décor, and once inside, are graciously invited to shop in an elegant setting amidst crystal chandeliers, Old-World stone floors, and an array of tantalizing scents packaged in vintage glass bottles. The coveted signature perfumes and handmade soaps are all produced locally and make beautiful gifts and tokens to take home after your trip. Steeped in a rich family history, Maison Godet is currently owned and operated by Sonia Godet, who has brought back to life her great-grandfather's perfume business after its long dormancy. Growing up near Grasse, the epicenter of the French perfume industry, Sonia's natural talent for making legendary perfumes seems to run in the family. After learning how to create exceptional perfumes and working abroad for several prestigious brands, including Cartier, Burberry, and Lancôme, she returned to the South of France to create exquisite scents and soaps that are all inspired by the original family brand.

Whether you are an art and antiques buyer scouting the exceptional wares available to professionals only at Béziers Antique Trade Market or a casual first-time browser searching for that special keepsake at the legendary *brocante* of Villeneuve-lès-Avignon, the extraordinary flea market venues throughout the South of France offer a gratifying experience that is sure to live in your memories for a lifetime. Here, an extraordinary hodgepodge of collectibles arranged in captivating vignettes draws flea market shoppers in for a closer look. A stunning mix of antique chairs strike a stylish pose that is sure to attract curious shoppers. Other eye-catching finds include gorgeous handmade scarves, old baskets, and tables of beautiful vintage linens that include anything from full sets of crisp monogrammed napkins to charming French dish towels and sun-faded tablecloths.

LEFT: Collectors of authentic Old-World furniture will relish in the regal trappings they can uncover during the hunt. Opulent treasures to be found at the fleas include elaborately carved antique commodes paired with tall, stately mirrors and lovely accessories, such as ormolu clocks, antique Chinese porcelain urns, quirky deer head wall mounts, wonderfully aged patina candlesticks, and extraordinary well-worn Aubusson rugs.

RIGHT: Boxes and bins of curious finds discovered along the streets and hidden pathways of the flea markets are very much a part of the magic of shopping in the South of France. Browsers can pick through tables and baskets of eclectic potpourri, including this collection of playing cards and board game pieces, and a spectacular cache of gilded frames and wooden embellishments.

The crowded sidewalk displays at the fleas are brimming with unexpected treasures, such as this impressive assortment of antique watering cans. Both serious antiques aficionados and casual browsers alike can easily while away an entire day sifting through the endless array of quirky curiosities. While strolling through the winding cobblestone streets, visitors to the outdoor flea markets can seek out rare finds, including elegant vintage tablecloths, beautiful hand-stitched coverlets, and other whimsical handmade textiles. From vintage Old-World globes and tableware to extraordinary framed butterfly collections, prized china pieces, and charming kitchen canister sets, the shops and flea markets of Provence and the surrounding countryside offer a virtual paradise for those who love the hunt.

Along the streets, casually elegant displays of the unexpected seem to capture spot-on the artful nonchalance and decided je ne sais quoi of French style. Here, a collection of antique cameras poised alongside old photographs and other vintage ephemera will surely catch the eye of an interested buyer before day's end. An artful display of shelved curios makes a stunning focal point for this street display flanked with old picture frames, stone statuary, and other captivating pieces of architectural salvage. A single antique chair paired with a matching side table strikes an elegant pose beside a storefront window.

Provence and the surrounding countryside offer an abundance of market streets that sell an incredible selection of fresh flowers and seasonal produce, and L'Isle-sur-la-Sorgue is certainly no exception to the rule. Shoppers will not be disappointed with the exceptional variety of freshly baked pastries and just-picked floral bouquets. Throughout the year, visitors flock to these open-air farmers' markets for the best selection of fruits, vegetables, and other irresistible farm-to-table offerings. Buckets brimming with fresh-cut roses, hydrangeas, and other colorful blooms will undoubtedly be picked over in the early morning hours while still at their peak. Vibrant clusters of freshly cut tulips entice shoppers passing by to pick up a beautiful bouquet for home.

RESOURCES

French Country
Editor: Cindy Smith Cooper
Senior Art Director: Tracy Wood Franklin
Senior Copy Editor: Rhonda Lee Lother

Cover: Photography by Ton Bouwer

Introduction, 8–11: Text by Jeanne Delathouder.

Keeping the Character, 14–31: Photography by Jody Stewart; text by Celia Rufey.

French Flavor, 32–41: Photography by Colleen Duffley; text by Jeanne Delathouder.

Old Farm, New Life, 42–55: Photography by Ton Bouwer; text and styling by Monique van der Pauw. Ceramics by Dutch artist Ine Schoots, ineschootskeramiek.nl.

French Love Affair, 56–69: Photography by Robert Sanderson; text and styling by Maggie Colvin; Oka, okadirect.com; David Swanson Antiques, davidswansonantiques.co.uk; Mark Wilkinson, markwilkinsonkitchens.com; Barbara Coupe, barbaracoupe.co.uk; Farrow and Ball, farrow-ball.com; Chelsea Textiles, 0207 584 4844; Alexander Interiors, alexanderinteriorsltd.co.uk.

Movers and Shakers, 70–83: Photography by Jody Stewart; text by Celia Rufey; Polly Lyster indigo and vegetable-dyed antique linens, dyeworks.co.uk; architectural antiques, Frères Labrouche, labrouche.com; sofas are covered in Linara by Romo, romo.com; cushions are in embroidered and check fabrics by Chelsea Textiles, chelseatextiles.com; bedcover made in fabric by Robert Kime, robertkime.com, antique nursing chair covered in Castang Basket by Brocante Fabrics, brocantefabrics.co.uk.

Château de Christin, 84–103: Photography by Robert Sanderson; text by Penny Botting. All furniture handed down by family. Bedroom painted in "Borrowed Light" in Estate; Herbalist Room painted in "Lichen," Estate Emulsion; upstairs landing painted in "Book Room Red," Estate Emulsion, from Farrow & Ball, farrow-ball.com; glass storage jars from Divertimenti, divertimenti.co.uk.

Champagne Chic, 104–119: Photography by Ton Bouwer, moonshineweb.eu; production, styling and text by Monique van der Pauw; armchairs, maisonsdumonde.com; fabrics in Muscari and Pivoine from Marché St. Pierre, marchesaintpierre.com; fabrics in Seringat and breakfast room made of old embroidered sheets, bought at antiques shops and markets; bedlinens from Blanc d'Ivoire blancdivoire.com; crockery from Côté Table, cote-table.com.

Vintage Passion, 122–133: Photography by Tria Giovan; text by Lauren Eberle; interior design by Donna Brown with a consultation by Pamela Pierce, ppiercedesigns.com; contractor, Donna Brown, graydoorantiques.com; collage by Ida Kohlmeyer.

Lovely Legacy, 134–145: Photography by Laurey Glenn; text by Cindy Smith Cooper; styling by Kim Chiselko; interior design by Pandy Agnew, pandyagnewinteriors.com; original art in foyer and living room by Jane Ingols.

French Coup de Coeur, 146–153: Photography by Anice Hoachlander, hdphoto.com; text by Jeanne Delathouder; architect: Anthony "Ankie" Barnes, Barnes Vanze Architects, 202-337-7255, barnesvanze.com; landscape architects, Leslie Gignoux and Scott Fritz, Fritz & Gignoux Landscape Architects,

202-244-2016, fritzgignoux.com; custom kitchen cabinetry and library built-ins, Timothy Rowe and Andrew Krochak, Heartwood Design, 434-361-1262, ext. 102, heartwoodkitchens.com; interior design consultation: Carolyn Wilson and Elizabeth Boland, Design in a Day, wilsonbolanddesign.com; reclaimed flooring and beams, Ben Cochran, Cochran's Lumber, 540-533-1061, cochranslumber.com; specialty painting for kitchen, windows and doors: Billet Collins, 301-670-5550, billetcollins.com.

Rustic French Allure, 154–165: Photography by Colleen Duffley; text by Jeanne Delathouder; Château Domingue, 3560 West 12th Street, Houston, Texas 77008, chateaudomingue.com; Pamela Pierce, Pierce Designs & Associates, 713-961-7540, ppiercedesigns.com.

Attention to Detail, 166–179: Photography by Lauren Rubenstein; text by Bethany Adams; architect: Yong Pak, Pak-Heydt & Associates, 404-231-3195, pakheydt.com; light fixtures in living room from Currey & Company, 877-768-6428, curreycodealers.com; backsplash tile from Renaissance Tile & Bath, 855-395-9677, renaissancetileandbath.com; dining room chairs from Duralee, 800-275-3872, duralee.com; custom by Hood-Charles Calhoun, blacksmith, 404-755-6155, calhounmetalworks.com

Signature Style, 180–195: Photography by Colleen Duffley; text by Lauren Eberle.

Treasures & Antiques, 198–215: Photography by Colleen Duffley; text by Jeanne Delathouder.